THE
PATROITS

INTRODUCTION

A glance to your left at the superb Colin Wright painting of 5551 is the reason for producing this book, the profits of which will go directly to the completion of the building of *The Unknown Warrior*. As depicted in the painting the locomotive will be outshopped in crimson lake livery, this being voted for by the membership of The LMS-Patriot Project. We are striving to complete the build in the not too distant future.

I joined the Project in 2011 and produced my first membership newsletter (Warrior No. 17) in February 2013. At that time the number of Patriot photos we held was fairly low, but over the ensuing five years, through appeals in The Warrior and the generosity of many people including some top class photographers, our library has increased immensely with many of the images never having been published before. So rather than just storing them on a computer the idea came to me to produce a fund-raising pictorial book that serves as a record of each member of this much missed class of locomotive in their original parallel boiler form. The amount of images the Project now possess is the reason that this book features the first 26 locomotives of the class, 45500–45525, forming Volume 1, with 45526–45551 to follow at a later date.

Finally, I would like to thank your for purchasing this book and helping the Project towards completion of *The Unknown Warrior*. I hope that looking through the pages of this book gives you as much pleasure as it did me putting it together. If you're not a member of The LMS-Patriot Project but would like to know more please refer to the contact details on the back cover.

Best wishes
Pete Sikes
The LMS-Patriot Project

The LMS-Patriot Project
CREATING THE NEW NATIONAL MEMORIAL ENGINE

THE
PATRIOTS

FOREWORD BY DAVID BRADSHAW

The LMS Patriots were the first modern express passenger locomotives produced entirely by the recently formed London Midland and Scottish Railway, unlike the closely related Royal Scots which were jointly designed by the North British Locomotive Company and Derby Works of the LMS. Originally designated 'Rebuilt Claughtons' because they were originally conceived as a rebuild of Bowen Cooke's LNWR four cylinder 4-6-0s, utilising that design's larger boiler designated G9½"S, they were in reality smaller boilered Royal Scots and proved to be better performers as well as being much more economical and reliable than the Claughtons. The first two did include some parts from withdrawn Claughtons but the remainder were to all intents and purposes new engines.

Before going into series production William Stanier joined the LMS from the Great Western and made some strategic changes to the design, in particular to the axleboxes which undoubtedly improved their performance. Fifty two locomotives were built to Sir Henry Fowler's design between 1930 and 1934 and proved to be a most satisfactory design, doing all that was required of them over the 30 plus years of their main line service. Such was the robustness of the chassis design that 18 were rebuilt with the larger 2A boiler and in this guise were treated as the equivalent to the Royal Scot.

As a pupil at Wellington Grammar School Shropshire in the fifties, I first made the acquaintance of the class when one of my classmates mentioned that he had seen an engine called *Bradshaw* in Wellington station on a Stafford local service. From that point on I was hooked and over the next few years I saw all 52 members of the class.

Like many others I was deeply disappointed when not one member of the class was preserved and following the announcement by the GWS that they were to build the 78th member of the Saint class, I harboured thoughts of building a 53rd Patriot, initially using the remains of Barry Scrapyard wreck No. 45699 *Galatea*. It soon became evident that whist the two designs were similar, there were sufficient differences to make this impractical. The completion of the first full new build, A1 Pacific No. 60163 *Tornado*, convinced me that a new Patriot was feasible and in August 2007 an article putting forward the idea was published in Steam Railway and following its publication considerable support was forthcoming, confirming my belief that the Patriots had a special place in the hearts of LMS enthusiasts. In the intervening years that support has increased to the point that we expect the locomotive to be in steam during the Autumn of 2019 and running on the main line during 2020.

In order to make this dream a reality we need to continue fund-raising at the levels achieved to date. I am sure part 1 of this series will be a great success illustrating as it does the first 26 members of the class. I invite anyone interested in LMS steam to join this wonderful project without delay. Details as to how you can help are found on the back cover of this book. With your help and support, completion of No. 5551 *The Unknown Warrior* is within our reach.

David Bradshaw
Chairman, The LMS-Patriot Project

THE
PATRIOTS

SPECIFICATIONS

Designer	*Sir Henry Fowler*	Wheelbase (inc. tender)	*54ft 4in*
Built	*1930–1934*	Overall Length (inc. tender)	*62ft 8½in*
Builder	*Crewe and Derby Works*	Parallel Boiler	*5ft 5½in diameter*
Purpose	*Express Passenger*	Boiler Pressure	*200psi*
Wheel Arrangement	*4-6-0*	Cylinders	*Three at 18in x 26in*
Weight (locomotive)	*80 tons 15 cwt*	Tractive Effort	*26,520lbs*
Weight (tender)	*42 tons 15 cwt*	Number in class	*52*
Front Bogie Wheels	*3ft 3in*	Coal Capacity	*5 tons 10 cwt*
Driving Wheels	*6ft 9in*	Water Capacity	*3,500 gallons*

ACKNOWLEDGEMENTS

Written, compiled and edited in 2018 by The LMS-Patriot Company Limited. © The LMS-Patriot Company Limited.

Thanks to the following for supplying photographs: Chris Tasker (for scanning and supplying many Patriot photographs acquired by the Manchester Locomotive Society), Brian Stephenson (Rail Stephenson Archive), Robin Fell (The Transport Treasury), Paul Chancellor (Colour-Rail), Edward Talbot Collection, Bill Ashcroft, Gordon Coltas Trust, David Anderson, Frank Cassell, Richard Smithies, John J. G. Wilson (courtesy of Alan Inckle), Dick Blenkinsop, Chris Banks and Colin Walker.

Thanks also to George Green of Irwell Press for permission to use information contained within
The Book of the Patriot 4-6-0s by Ian Sixsmith, published by Irwell Press Limited.

45500
Patriot

LMS Number (pre-/post 1934)	5971/5500
Date Built/Where	8th November 1930/Derby
Date Renamed	25th February 1937
Total Mileage	1,239,904
Withdrawn	Newton Heath/March 1961
Scrapped	April 1961/Crewe Works

Rebuilt from LNWR Claughton No. 5971 Croxteth.

The name Patriot was originally carried by LNWR Claughton No. 1914 in memory of their employees who lost their lives during the First World War.

△
No. 5971 *Croxteth* pictured on an express working through Essendine in the early to mid-1930s.
PHOTO: THE TRANSPORT TREASURY.

◁
No. 5500 *Patriot* at Camden shed in c.1936.
PHOTO: C. R. L. COLES/RAIL ARCHIVE STEPHENSON.

No. 45550 *Patriot* is seen bedecked with Remembrance Day poppies in November 1960. The locomotive is standing on Mill Road bridge having been especially loaned to Rugby shed by 26A Newton Heath shed for the occasion.

PHOTO: BRUCE CHAPMAN/COLOUR-RAIL.COM

The original *Patriot* nameplate forms part of the War Memorial at Rugby Depot.

PHOTO: OAKWOOD VISUALS.

No. 45500 *Patriot* passes through Wilmslow on 17th May 1951.
PHOTO: T. LEWIS.
© MANCHESTER LOCOMOTIVE SOCIETY/THE LMS-PATRIOT PROJECT.

No. 45500 *Patriot* double heads a freight through Ulverston on 12th November 1958 with Fowler 4F 0-6-0 No. 44461.
PHOTO: BILL ASHCROFT. © THE LMS-PATRIOT PROJECT.

The leader of the class, No. 45500 *Patriot* pictured on the West Coast Main Line near Symington with a Liverpool/Manchester to Glasgow express on 25th June 1960. Note the driving wheels with large centre bosses inherited from the LNWR 'Claughton' class loco it replaced.
PHOTO: DAVID ANDERSON. © THE LMS-PATRIOT PROJECT.

45501

St. Dunstan's

LMS Number (pre-/post-1934)	5902/5501
Date Built/Where	13th November 1930/Derby
Date Renamed	17th April 1937
Total Mileage	1,266,776
Withdrawn	August 1961
Scrapped	September 1961/Crewe Works

Rebuilt from LNWR Claughton No. 5902 Sir Frank Ree, the name which it carried until 1937.

Renamed St. Dunstan's after the School for the Blind which was founded in 1915 for those blinded in the First World War.

△
No. 45501 *St. Dunstan's* pictured at Crewe Works
on 17th August 1958.
PHOTO: P. HUTCHINSON.
© MANCHESTER LOCOMOTIVE SOCIETY/THE LMS-PATRIOT PROJECT.

◁
No. 45501 *St. Dunstan's* at Betley Road on 8th August 1959.
PHOTO: A. C. GILBERT.
© MANCHESTER LOCOMOTIVE SOCIETY/THE LMS-PATRIOT PROJECT.

No. 45501 *St. Dunstan's* storms through
Handforth on 1st March 1953.

PHOTO: T. LEWIS.
© MANCHESTER LOCOMOTIVE SOCIETY/
THE LMS-PATRIOT PROJECT.

No. 45501 *St. Dunstan's* at Levenshulme, 15th June 1957.
PHOTO: R. E. GEE. © MANCHESTER LOCOMOTIVE SOCIETY/THE LMS-PATRIOT PROJECT.

45502
Royal Naval Division

LMS Number (pre-/post-1934)	5959/5502
Date Built/Where	*July 1932/Crewe*
Date Named	*5th June 1937*
Total Mileage	*1,388,595*
Withdrawn	*September 1960*
Scrapped	*October 1960/Crewe Works*

The Royal Naval Division was formed at the outbreak of the First World War from Royal Navy and Royal Marine reservists and volunteers not needed for service at sea.

The first of the class to be withdrawn.

△
A pre-1937 shot of No. 5502 at an unknown location.
PHOTO COURTESY PETER SIKES. © **THE LMS-PATRIOT PROJECT.**

◁
No. 45502 *Royal Naval Division* passes through Lancaster Castle Station on freight duties, date unknown.
PHOTO: BILL ASHCROFT. © **THE LMS-PATRIOT PROJECT.**

45503 *The Royal Leicestershire Regiment*

LMS Number (pre-/post-1934)	5985/5503
Date Built/Where	July 1932/Crewe
Date Renamed	3rd November 1948
Total Mileage	1,265,281
Withdrawn	August 1961
Scrapped	September 1961/Crewe Works

Engine named The Leicestershire Regiment from 8th July 1938.

The Leicestershire Regiment (Royal Leicestershire Regiment after 1946) was a line infantry regiment of the British Army, with a history going back to 1688. The regiment saw service for three centuries, in numerous wars and conflicts such as both World War I and World War II, before being amalgamated, in September 1964, to form the present day Royal Anglian Regiment.

No. 45503 *The Royal Leicestershire Regiment* calls at Syston station while hauling the 5.32pm from Peterborough to Leicester on 17th May 1960. The splendid gantry controlling the south junction can be seen behind the train.

PHOTO: © FRANK CASSELL.

◁
No. 45503 *The Royal Leicestershire Regiment* on a light engine movement at Preston in 1961.

PHOTO: BILL ASHCROFT. © THE LMS-PATRIOT PROJECT.

No. 45503 *The Royal Leicestershire Regiment* departs
Preston working a banana train on 2nd August 1960.
PHOTO: BILL ASHCROFT. © THE LMS-PATRIOT PROJECT.

No. 45503 *The Royal Leicestershire Regiment* at Dalry Road, Edinburgh on 14th July 1955.
The engine was there due to working a through summer timetable service
between Birmingham (New Street) and Edinburgh (Princes Street) with the return
working on the following morning. Normally worked by a Crewe North (5A) based
engine and on this occasion unusually brought an original Patriot to Edinburgh.
The background appearance of a Caledonian Railway 3F 0-6-0 confirms that it is the
Scottish Region. This whole area has now disappeared, making way for the western
approach road into the Scottish capital.

PHOTO: DAVID ANDERSON. © THE LMS-PATRIOT PROJECT.

45504 *Royal Signals*

LMS Number (pre-/post-1934)	*5987/5504*
Date Built/Where	*July 1932/Crewe*
Date Named	*10th April 1937*
Total Mileage	*1,274,026*
Withdrawn	*March 1962*
Scrapped	*March 1962/Crewe Works*

The Royal Signals are the Army's communicators. Formed when a Royal Warrant for the creation of a Corps of Signals was signed by the Secretary of State for War, Winston Churchill, on 28 June 1920.

No. 45505 *The Royal Army Ordnance Corps* passes through Madeley in the summer of 1959.

PHOTO: J. D. DARBY.
© MANCHESTER LOCOMOTIVE SOCIETY/THE LMS-PATRIOT PROJECT.

45505

The Royal Army Ordnance Corps

LMS Number (pre-/post-1934)	*5949/5505*
Date Built/Where	*July 1932/Crewe*
Date Named	*8th August 1947*
Mileage to end of 1961	*1,362,858*
Withdrawn	*May 1962*
Scrapped	*August 1962/Crewe Works*

Allocated the name Wemyss Bay during the war years (1939-1945) but not applied.

The Royal Army Ordnance Corps (RAOC) was a corps of the British Army. It dealt only with the supply and maintenance of weaponry, munitions and other military equipment until 1965.

△
No. 45505 *The Royal Army Ordnance Corps* works a
fitted freight through Thrimby Grange, Penrith on 16th May 1961.

No. 45505 *The Royal Army Ordnance Corps* ascends
Miles Platting Bank, Manchester, date unknown.
© MANCHESTER LOCOMOTIVE SOCIETY/THE LMS-PATRIOT PROJECT.
▽

45506 *The Royal Pioneer Corps*

LMS Number (pre-/post-1934)	5974/5506
Date Built/Where	August 1932/Crewe
Date Named	15th September 1948
Total Mileage	1,286,842
Withdrawn	March 1962
Scrapped	March 1962/Crewe Works

The Royal Pioneer Corps was a British Army combatant corps used for light engineering tasks. It was formed in 1939 and amalgamated into the Royal Logistic Corps in 1993.

No. 5506 at Standish, near Wigan on 18th May 1948.
PHOTO: N. FIELDS.
© MANCHESTER LOCOMOTIVE SOCIETY/THE LMS-PATRIOT PROJECT.

No. 45506 *The Royal Pioneer Corps* makes a
positioning move at Bangor in 1951.
PHOTO: GORDON COLTAS TRUST.
© MANCHESTER LOCOMOTIVE SOCIETY/THE LMS-PATRIOT PROJECT.

△

No. 45506 *The Royal Pioneer Corps* passes through Preston on a Carlisle to Warrington fitted freight, date unknown.

PHOTO: BILL ASHCROFT. © THE LMS-PATRIOT PROJECT.

◁

No. 45506 *The Royal Pioneer Corps* passes through picturesque Dore and Totley in the early 1960s. Note the smiling driver and young spotter about to note the engine number.

PHOTO: © MANCHESTER LOCOMOTIVE SOCIETY/THE LMS-PATRIOT PROJECT.

◁
No. 45506 *The Royal Pioneer Corps* makes a robust effort up Lickey Incline with the Fridays Only 10.20am Bristol Temple Meads to Sheffield service on 5th August 1960. At this time 45506 was allocated to Bristol Barrow Road (82E) along with 45504 and 45519.
PHOTO: COLIN WALKER. © MARTIN WALKER.

△
No. 45506 *The Royal Pioneer Corps* working a fitted freight passes Penrith signal box on 13th August 1950. The sixth vehicle in the train appears to be a GW Toad brake van with the guard looking out.
PHOTO: N. FIELDS.
© MANCHESTER LOCOMOTIVE SOCIETY/THE LMS-PATRIOT PROJECT.

45507
Royal Tank Corps

LMS Number (pre-/post-1934)	*5936/5507*
Date Built/Where	*August 1932/Crewe*
Date Named	*20th November 1937*
Mileage to end of 1960	*1,280,948*
Withdrawn	*May 1962*
Scrapped	*March 1963/Horwich Works*

The Royal Tank Regiment is the oldest tank unit in the world, being formed by the British Army in 1916 during the Great War. Today, it is the armoured regiment of the British Army's 1st Armoured Infantry Brigade.

◁
No. 45507 *Royal Tank Corps* passing Salts Mill, Saltaire, Bradford. Salts Mill is a former textile mill, now an art gallery, shopping centre and restaurant complex.
PHOTO: RICHARD SMITHIES. © THE LMS-PATRIOT PROJECT.

△
In a pre-1937 shot No. 5507 is pictured on shed, location unknown.
PHOTO COURTESY PETE SIKES.
© THE LMS-PATRIOT PROJECT.

No. 45507 *Royal Tank Corps* works an express through
Standon Bridge, Staffordshire on 19th April 1957.

PHOTO: T. LEWIS.
© MANCHESTER LOCOMOTIVE SOCIETY/THE LMS-PATRIOT PROJECT.

No. 45507 *Royal Tank Corps*
pictured in store at
Preston Shed on
5th August 1962.

PHOTO: BILL ASHCROFT.
© **THE LMS-PATRIOT PROJECT.**

45508

LMS Number (pre-/post-1934)	6010/5508
Date Built/Where	August 1932/Crewe
Year Named	–
Total Mileage	1,259,416
Withdrawn	December 1960
Scrapped	December 1960/Crewe Works

In 1956 British Railways chose 45508 to be fitted with an experimental draughting system which gave the engine a look which was out of keeping with its previous handsome appearance due to the addition of a hideously shaped stove pipe chimney known as 'the bucket', which it kept until withdrawal. The experiment did little to increase the steam raising capacity and certainly did nothing to improve the look of the engine.

▷

Two unnamed Patriots, Nos. 5508 and 5510 pass Oxenholme signal box, date unknown.

PHOTO: © MANCHESTER LOCOMOTIVE SOCIETY/ THE LMS-PATRIOT PROJECT.

△
No. 45508 waits departure time from Carlisle Citadel
on 15th September 1960.
PHOTO: © GORDON COLTAS TRUST/
MANCHESTER LOCOMOTIVE SOCIETY/THE LMS-PATRIOT PROJECT.

◁
No. 45508 at Carlisle Citadel station, 21st May 1960.
PHOTO: JOHN J. G. WILSON. © ALAN INCKLE.

No. 45508, fitted with stove pipe chimney, is pictured at Skew Bridge, Preston on W254, 10.50 ex-Workington in 1959.

PHOTO: BILL ASHCROFT. © THE LMS-PATRIOT PROJECT.

No. 45508, with its ugly spout for a chimney,
passes through Madeley in the summer of 1959.
PHOTO: J. D. DARBY.
© MANCHESTER LOCOMOTIVE SOCIETY/THE LMS-PATRIOT PROJECT.

45509
The Derbyshire Yeomanry

LMS Number (pre-/post-1934)	*6005/5509*
Date Built/Where	*August 1932/Crewe*
Date Named	*10th November 1951*
Total Mileage	*1,249,852*
Withdrawn	*August 1961*
Scrapped	*September 1961/Crewe Works*

Allocated the name Commando during the war years (1939-1945)
but not applied.

The Derbyshire Yeomanry was a yeomanry regiment of the British Army,
first raised in 1794, which served as a cavalry regiment and dismounted infantry
regiment in the First World War and provided two reconnaissance regiments in the
Second World War. In 1957 it was amalgamated with the Leicestershire Yeomanry
to form the Leicestershire and Derbyshire (Prince Albert's Own) Yeomanry.

◁
An evocative scene as No. 45509 *The Derbyshire Yeomanry*
is pictured in the early morning mist at Gloucester Eastgate
with a Birmingham New Street to Bristol service on
18th November 1953.
PHOTO: DICK BLENKINSOP. © THE LMS-PATRIOT PROJECT.

No. 45509 *The Derbyshire Yeomanry*
departs Preston for Manchester, 1958.
PHOTO: BILL ASHCROFT. © THE LMS-PATRIOT PROJECT.

No. 45509 *The Derbyshire Yeomanry* arrives at Preston working a Manchester to Blackpool train on 6th May 1959.
PHOTO: BILL ASHCROFT. © THE LMS-PATRIOT PROJECT.

A timeless scene sees No. 45509 *The Derbyshire Yeomanry* departing from Millers Dale and passing 4F No. 44072 running tender first with a mixed freight on 24th June 1961.

PHOTO: N. FIELDS.
© MANCHESTER LOCOMOTIVE SOCIETY/THE LMS-PATRIOT PROJECT.

No. 45510 departs from Llandudno with a returning holiday excursion in June 1963.

1Z83

45510

45510

LMS Number (pre-/post-1934)	*6012/5510*
Date Built/Where	*August 1932/Crewe*
Year Named	*–*
Mileage to end of 1960	*1,301,202*
Withdrawn	*May 1962*
Scrapped	*August 1962/Crewe Works*

△
No. 6012 at an unknown
location, c.1932.
**PHOTO: W. H. WHITWORTH/
RAIL ARCHIVE STEPHENSON.**

No. 45510 at Crewe North Shed on 30th June 1951.

No. 45510 arrives at Lancaster Castle station working
a Barrow to Manchester service on 18th July 1961.
PHOTO: BILL ASHCROFT. © THE LMS-PATRIOT PROJECT.

45511 *Isle of Man*

LMS Number (pre-/post-1934)	5942/5511
Date Built/Where	August 1932/Crewe
Year Named	1938
Total Mileage	1,290,459
Withdrawn	February 1961
Scrapped	March 1961/Crewe Works

Named after the Isle of Man, the self-governing British Crown dependency in the Irish Sea between the islands of Great Britain and Ireland.

No. 5511 *Isle of Man* is pictured at Bangor shed on 28th March 1948. 70 years on from this photograph one of the nameplates from this fine locomotive was sold for £26,000.

PHOTO: © MANCHESTER LOCOMOTIVE SOCIETY/ THE LMS-PATRIOT PROJECT.

▽

A pair of LMS Patriot 4-6-0s Nos. 45511 *Isle of Man* and 45524 *Blackpool* climb Shap towards Scout Green with a Manchester to Glasgow express in 1949.
PHOTO: F. R. HEBRON/RAIL ARCHIVE STEPHENSON.

No. 45511 *Isle of Man* is seen on a freight working at Northampton on 9th July 1957.
PHOTO: © COLOUR-RAIL.COM

45512
Bunsen

LMS Number (pre-/post-1934)	5966/5512
Date Built/Where	September 1932/Crewe
Year Named	1932
Mileage to end of 1960	1,594,977
Date Rebuilt	July 1948
Withdrawn	March 1965
Scrapped	July 1965/Wishaw

Thought to be named after the inventor of the gas 'Bunsen Burner',
German chemist Robert Wilhelm Bunsen.

No. 5512 *Bunsen* awaits departure time from Nottingham Midland with an excursion thought to be heading for Wembley on 29th June, 1939.
PHOTO: JOHN P. WILSON/RAIL ARCHIVE STEPHENSON.

No. 5512 *Bunsen* on shed alongside Jubilee No. 5573 *Newfoundland*, with the Patriot having a 1A shed plate and the Jubilee 1B, the location could be either Willesden or Camden.
PHOTO COURTESY PETE SIKES. © THE LMS-PATRIOT PROJECT.
▽

△
No. 5512 *Bunsen* pictured at Basford Sand Sidings,
south of Crewe on 7th May 1959.

PHOTO: GEORGE BARLOW/THE TRANSPORT TREASURY.

◁
No. 5512 *Bunsen* near with Whitmore with a
Euston to Liverpool express c.1938.

PHOTO: RAIL ARCHIVE STEPHENSON.

45513

LMS Number (pre-/post-1934)	5958/5513
Date Built/Where	September 1932/Crewe
Year Named	–
Total Mileage	1,462,093
Withdrawn	September 1962
Scrapped	October 1962/Crewe Works

*Allocated the name Sir W. A. Stanier during the war years (1939-1945)
but not applied. The name was later allocated to Coronation class No. 46256 as
Sir William A. Stanier F.R.S.*

△
No. 5513 pictured c.1937 at an unknown location.
PHOTO COURTESY PETE SIKES. © THE LMS-PATRIOT PROJECT.

◁
No. 5513 works a Down express to Manchester
and is photographed near Polesworth, Warwickshire
on 21st June 1937.
PHOTO: GEORGE BARLOW/THE TRANSPORT TREASURY.

No. 45513 passes Balshaw Lane signal box working the 06.30 Carlisle to Crewe service in 1958.
PHOTO: BILL ASHCROFT. © THE LMS-PATRIOT PROJECT.

No. 45513 is removed from a down express at
Barrow-in-Furness at 6.25pm on 11th September 1961.
PHOTO: PETER BLAND, COURTESY OF BRYAN CROSS.
© THE LMS-PATRIOT PROJECT.

Unnamed Patriot No. 45513 is seen departing
Lancaster Castle in the early 1960s.
PHOTO: © MANCHESTER LOCOMOTIVE SOCIETY/THE LMS-PATRIOT PROJECT.

45514
Holyhead

No 5983 climbs away from Nottingham London Road Junction towards Edwalton with the Up 'Thames-Forth Express' express for St. Pancras c.1933.

PHOTO: T. G. HEPBURN/RAIL ARCHIVE STEPHENSON

LMS Number (pre-/post-1934)	*5983/5514*
Date Built/Where	*September 1932/Crewe*
Date Named	*March 1947**
Total Mileage	*1,507,446*
Date Rebuilt	*March 1947*
Withdrawn	*May 1961*
Scrapped	*June 1961/Crewe Works*

*Named briefly in 1938 and then permanently after rebuilding in March 1947. The first rebuilt Patriot withdrawn from service.

Named after the town of Holyhead on Holy Island to the west of Anglesey which was the western terminus of the LMS for their cross-channel Irish passenger, freight and mail services.

No. 5983 climbs away from Nottingham past Edwalton
brick works with an Up express for St. Pancras c.1933.

PHOTO: T. G. HEPBURN/RAIL ARCHIVE STEPHENSON.

△
No. 5514 departs Birmingham New Street on 7th May 1938.
PHOTO: COURTESY CHRIS BANKS.

No. 5514 *Holyhead* passes through
Madeley on 19th May 1945.

PHOTO: J. D. DARBY.
© MANCHESTER LOCOMOTIVE SOCIETY/
THE LMS-PATRIOT PROJECT.

45515

Caernarvon

LMS Number (pre-/post-1934)	*5992/5515*
Date Built/Where	*September 1932/Crewe*
Date Named	*15th January 1939*
Mileage to end of 1961	*1,349,670*
Withdrawn	*June 1962*
Scrapped	*August 1962/Crewe Works*

Named after the town overlooking the southern end of the Menai Strait on the former LMS line between Bangor and Pwhelli, famous for its imposing Castle.

No. 45515 *Caernarvon* attracts the attention of a group of young spotters at Lancaster Castle, date unknown
PHOTO: RICHARD SMITHIES. © THE LMS-PATRIOT PROJECT.

◁
45515 *Caernarvon* departs Manchester Exchange with a parcels working, date unknown.
PHOTO: J. DAVENPORT.
© MANCHESTER LOCOMOTIVE SOCIETY/THE LMS-PATRIOT PROJECT.

Looking towards Vicars Bridge No. 45515 *Caernarvon* is pictured passing through the East Lancs platforms at Preston Station on a Southport to Blackpool train on 4th July 1960.

PHOTO: BILL ASHCROFT. © THE LMS-PATRIOT PROJECT.

No. 45515 *Caernarvon* double-heads with Britannia Class Pacific No. 70051 *Firth of Forth* at Skew Bridge, Preston on a Manchester to Glasgow express in 1959.

PHOTO: BILL ASHCROFT. © THE LMS-PATRIOT PROJECT.

No. 45515 *Caernarvon* works an express at Shap Wells
on 25th June 1960.

PHOTO: A. GILBERT.
© MANCHESTER LOCOMOTIVE SOCIETY/THE LMS-PATRIOT PROJECT.

No. 45515 *Caernarvon* pictured at York shed, recoaled and ready for a return trip to Liverpool in June 1961.

PHOTO: M. THOMPSON. © COLOUR-RAIL.COM

No. 45515 *Caernarvon* is captured at a grimy and neglected Manchester Victoria on 23rd September 1961.

PHOTO: © COLOUR-RAIL.COM

45516
The Bedfordshire and Hertfordshire Regiment

LMS Number (pre-/post-1934)	5982/5516
Date Built/Where	October 1932/Crewe
Date Named	31st July 1938
Total Mileage	1,330,644
Withdrawn	July 1961
Scrapped	September 1961/Crewe Works

The longest name of the Patriot class totalling 39 letters.

The Bedfordshire and Hertfordshire Regiment was the final title of a line infantry regiment of the British Army that was originally formed in 1688. After centuries of service in many small conflicts and wars, including both the First and Second World Wars, the regiment was amalgamated with the Essex Regiment in 1958 to form the 3rd East Anglian Regiment (16th/44th Foot). However this was short-lived and was amalgamated once again in 1964 with other regiments (including The Royal Leicestershire Regiment) to form the present Royal Anglian Regiment.

No. 45516 *The Bedfordshire and Hertfordshire Regiment* still in crimson lake livery with LMS on its tender but with British Railways numbering is pictured on shed at Preston in 1949. The engine was used in 1950 to haul a troop train from Southampton Docks carrying the men of the regiment it is named after.
PHOTO: THE TRANSPORT TREASURY.

No. 45516 *The Bedfordshire and Hertfordshire Regiment* awaits departure from Lancaster Castle sometime in the late 1950s.
PHOTO: © MANCHESTER LOCOMOTIVE SOCIETY/THE LMS-PATRIOT PROJECT.

△
No. 45516 *The Bedfordshire and Hertfordshire Regiment*
on shed at 8B Warrington (Dallam) on 6th May 1961.

PHOTO: JOHN J. G. WILSON. © ALAN INCKLE.

▷
45516 *The Bedfordshire and Hertfordshire Regiment* passes
Cheadle Hulme Signal Box on an Up express, date unknown.

PHOTO: T. LEWIS.
© MANCHESTER LOCOMOTIVE SOCIETY/THE LMS-PATRIOT PROJECT.

45517

LMS Number (pre-/post-1934)	5952/5517
Date Built/Where	February 1933/Crewe
Year Named	–
Mileage to end of 1960	1,295,802
Withdrawn	June 1962
Scrapped	July 1962/Crewe Works

◁
No. 45517 departs from Carlisle Citadel with a southbound working of 'The Waverley' on 16th April 1960.

PHOTO: © GORDON COLTAS TRUST/
MANCHESTER LOCOMOTIVE SOCIETY/THE LMS-PATRIOT PROJECT.

△
No. 45517 works light engine through Manchester Victoria
on 12th August 1960.

▷
45517 passes through Pendlebury Station in June 1951.

No. 45517 is seen climbing the gradient at Scout Green with Fowler 4P 2-6-4T No. 42424 banking on 29th July 1961.

PHOTO: N. FIELDS.
© MANCHESTER LOCOMOTIVE SOCIETY/
THE LMS-PATRIOT PROJECT.

No. 45517 climbs Beattock at Greskine with a northbound extra in July 1961.
PHOTO: W. J. VERDEN ANDERSON/RAIL ARCHIVE STEPHENSON.

No. 45517, one of the ten unnamed Patriots, is seen on Whitmore Troughs south of Crewe taking on water with an Up train on 3rd August 1957.
PHOTO: © DICK BLENKINSOP.

45518
Bradshaw

LMS Number (pre-/post-1934)	*6006/5518*
Date Built/Where	*February 1933/Crewe*
Date Named	*May 1939*
Mileage to August 1961	*1,355,270*
Withdrawn	*October 1962*
Scrapped	*February 1963/ Horwich Works*

The engine was named Bradshaw (briefly from May 1939 and again in early 1947) after the English cartographer, printer and publisher who is best known for developing the most successful and longest published series of combined railway timetables. George Bradshaw (1801-1853) has been brought to prominence by the Great British Railway Journey programmes presented by Michael Portillo.

△
LMS 'Patriot' No. 5518 is pictured on shed – date and location unknown, although taken before naming in 1939.
PHOTO COURTESY PETER SIKES. © THE LMS-PATRIOT PROJECT.

◁
No. 45518 *Bradshaw* sporting a mixture of LMS and BR liveries at Crewe on 21st June 1949.
PHOTO: THE TRANSPORT TREASURY.

△
No. 45518 *Bradshaw* at Hellifield on 10th March 1962.
PHOTO: N. FIELDS.
© MANCHESTER LOCOMOTIVE SOCIETY/THE LMS-PATRIOT PROJECT.

◁
A superb shot showing the power of the Patriots as
No. 45518 *Bradshaw* is pictured at the head an express
working. Although neither date or location were recorded
the shed code of 10B (Preston) would place it as being 1953
where it was allocated from 13th June to 19th September.
PHOTO: T. LEWIS.
© MANCHESTER LOCOMOTIVE SOCIETY/THE LMS-PATRIOT PROJECT.

45519
Lady Godiva

LMS Number (pre-/post-1934)	6008/5519	Total Mileage	1,366,224
Date Built/Where	*February 1933/Crewe*	Withdrawn	*March 1962*
Date Named	*February 1933*	Scrapped	*March 1962/Crewe Works*

No. 45519 *Lady Godiva* at
Crewe North Shed on 14th April 1957.

PHOTO: A. C. GILBERT.
© MANCHESTER LOCOMOTIVE SOCIETY/
THE LMS-PATRIOT PROJECT.
▽

Named after Godiva, Countess of Mercia in Old English Godgifu, who was an English noblewoman. According to a legend dating at least to the 13th century, she rode naked – covered only in her long hair – through the streets of Coventry to gain a remission of the oppressive taxation that her husband imposed on his tenants.

No. 45519 *Lady Godiva* pauses at Stockport Edgeley sometime in the 1950s.
PHOTO: N. HARROP.
© MANCHESTER LOCOMOTIVE SOCIETY/
THE LMS-PATRIOT PROJECT.

No. 45519 *Lady Godiva* pictured working an express in the late 1950s, location unknown.
PHOTO: © MANCHESTER LOCOMOTIVE SOCIETY/
THE LMS-PATRIOT PROJECT.

No. 45519 *Lady Godiva* tops up with water at Lichfield Trent Valley on 10th April 1960.
PHOTO: A. C. GILBERT. © MANCHESTER LOCOMOTIVE SOCIETY/THE LMS-PATRIOT PROJECT.

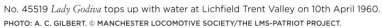

Barrow Road Patriot No. 45519 *Lady Godiva* takes water at Derby Midland with the northbound 'Devonian' on 11th July, 1959.
PHOTO: T. G. HEPBURN/RAIL ARCHIVE STEPHENSON.

45520 *Llandudno*

LMS Number (pre-/post-1934)	*5954/5520*
Date Built/Where	*February 1933/Crewe*
Year Named	*1937*
Total Mileage	*1,359,576*
Withdrawn	*May 1962*
Scrapped	*June 1962/Crewe Works*

Named after the seaside town of Llandudno in North Wales, located at the end of a 3 mile long branch line from Llandudno Junction on the Crewe to Holyhead North Wales Coast Line.

No. 5954 at Kentish Town Shed in April 1933.
PHOTO: EDWARD TALBOT COLLECTION.
▽

◁
No. 45520 *Llandudno*
storms past Slaithwaite
with a Hull to Liverpool
express in March 1951.
**PHOTO: KENNETH FIELD/
RAIL ARCHIVE STEPHENSON.**

No. 45520 *Llandudno* passes through Longsight
on 9th June 1951.

PHOTO: T. LEWIS.
© MANCHESTER LOCOMOTIVE SOCIETY/THE LMS-PATRIOT PROJECT.

No. 45520 *Llandudno* shortly after departure from
Manchester London Road on 21st February 1953.
Note that although only comprising four coaches the train is
being banked by what looks to be a Stanier 2-6-4 tank.

No. 5933 at Kentish Town shed on 2nd September, 1933.
PHOTO: C. R. GORDON STUART/RAIL ARCHIVE STEPHENSON.

45521
Rhyl

LMS Number (pre-/post-1934)	*5933/5521*
Date Built/Where	*March 1933/Derby*
Year Named	*1937*
Total Mileage	*1,602,958*
Withdrawn	*September 1963*
Scrapped	*November 1963/ Crewe Works*

Rhyl railway station is on the Crewe to Holyhead North Wales Coast Line and serves the holiday resort of Rhyl, Wales. The station was opened to traffic on 1st May 1848, being one of the original intermediate stations on the Chester and Holyhead Railway main line along the coast.

No. 5933 approaches Edwalton with a Glasgow to St. Pancras express in 1933.
PHOTO: T. G. HEPBURN/RAIL ARCHIVE STEPHENSON.

LMS Patriot 4-6-0 No 5521 passes Rugby
with an Up express c.1936.
PHOTO: T. G. HEPBURN/RAIL ARCHIVE STEPHENSON.

◁

Looking immaculate in original LMS livery, No. 5521 *Rhyl* prepares to depart Birmingham New Street on 17th May 1938.
PHOTO: © EDWARD TALBOT COLLECTION.

No. 5521 *Rhyl* pictured at Shrewsbury c.1934.
PHOTO COURTESY CHRIS BANKS.
▽

45522
Prestatyn

LMS Number (pre-/post-1934)	5973/5522
Date Built/Where	March 1933/Derby
Date Named	22nd March 1939
Mileage at end of 1960	1,533,492
Withdrawn	September 1964
Scrapped	June 1965/Wigan

Prestatyn is located on the North Wales Coast Line and the station there was opened in 1848. The coming of the railway is credited with bringing prosperity to the town, which at that time was an aspiring resort.

No. 5522 in the centre road at Nottingham Midland c.1935.
PHOTO: J. N. HALL/ RAIL ARCHIVE STEPHENSON.
▷

No. 5522 *Prestatyn* in grimy condition at Polmadie shed, Glasgow, date unknown but probably early 1940s.
PHOTO: J. ROBERTSON/THE TRANSPORT TREASURY.
▽

45523 *Bangor*

LMS Number (pre-/post-1934)	6026/5523
Date Built/Where	*March 1933/Crewe*
Date Named	*1938*
Mileage at end of 1960	*1,478,630*
Withdrawn	*January 1964*
Scrapped	*March 1964/Crewe Works*

Named after the oldest city in Wales, it is also one of the smallest cities in the United Kingdom. Bangor lies on the coast of North Wales near the Menai Strait.

No. 5523 at Leamington Spa Avenue in 1936, the engine wasn't named until 1938.

No. 5523 *Bangor* is pictured near Lancaster in 1938.

△
An atmospheric picture of No. 5523, not yet named, at Euston in June 1935.
PHOTO: THE TRANSPORT TREASURY.

No. 5523 *Bangor* with an Up train at Colwyn Bay in July 1939.

PHOTO: T. G. HEPBURN/RAIL ARCHIVE STEPHENSON.

45524
Blackpool

LMS Number (pre-/post-1934)	5907/5524
Date Built/Where	*March 1933/Crewe*
Date Renamed	*23rd March 1936*
Mileage at end of 1960	*1,270,093*
Withdrawn	*September 1962*
Scrapped	*October 1962/Crewe Works*

Original name Sir Frederick Harrison.

Named after the famous seaside resort on the Lancashire coast in North West England. The town is located on the Irish Sea, between the Ribble and Wyre estuaries.

▷

No. 5524 *Blackpool* with an unidentified sister-engine piloting arrive at Crewe on 19th May 1948.
PHOTO: N. FIELDS.
© MANCHESTER LOCOMOTIVE SOCIETY/THE LMS-PATRIOT PROJECT.

△
45524 *Blackpool* departs Crewe Station, date unknown.

△
45524 *Blackpool* passes through Vulcan Halt hauling a
mixed freight on 31st December 1960.

PHOTO: N. FIELDS.
© MANCHESTER LOCOMOTIVE SOCIETY/THE LMS-PATRIOT PROJECT.

45524 *Blackpool* passes Preston No. 5 signal box on a Euston to Barrow service on 25th September 1961.

PHOTO: BILL ASHCROFT. © THE LMS-PATRIOT PROJECT.

45525
Colwyn Bay

LMS Number (pre-/post-1934)	*5916/5525*
Date Built/Where	*March 1933/Derby*
Date Renamed	*1937*
Total Mileage	*1,469,953*
Withdrawn	*May 1963*
Scrapped	*June 1963/Crewe Works*

Originally named E. Tootal Broadhurst in 1933.

The town is situated about halfway along the north coast of Wales, between the sea and the Pwllycrochan Woods. Established as its own separate parish in 1844 with just a small grouping of homes and farms where the community of Old Colwyn stands today.

△
No. 5916 *E. Tootal Broadhurst* at
Nottingham Midland c.1934.
PHOTO: J. N. HALL/RAIL ARCHIVE STEPHENSON.

◁
No. 5525 at this time named *E. Tootal Broadhurst* in light
steam at Crewe North, although no date is available the
engine was renamed *Colwyn Bay* in 1937 so the photo must
pre-date this year.
**PHOTO: © MANCHESTER LOCOMOTIVE SOCIETY/
THE LMS-PATRIOT PROJECT.**

△

With the Boots factory dominating the skyline No. 5916 *E. Tootal Broadhurst* is seen at Nottingham Midland c.1933.

PHOTO: T. G. HEPBURN/RAIL ARCHIVE STEPHENSON.

△
No. 5525 arriving at Euston with an Up Cup Tie Special in
1938, possibly for the final which saw Preston North End
beat Huddersfield Town 1-0.
PHOTO: C. R. L. COLES/RAIL ARCHIVE STEPHENSON.